Built Around the Fire

Poems

Nathan Lipps

STEPHEN F. AUSTIN STATE UNIVERSITY PRESS

Production Manager: Kimberly Verhines
Book Design: Mallory LeCroy
Cover Design: Twotma (Aimée Pedezert)

ISBN: 978-1-62288-255-7

For more information:
Stephen F. Austin State University Press
P.O. Box 13007 SFA Station
Nacogdoches, Texas 75962
sfapress@sfasu.edu

Distributed by the Texas A&M University Press Book Consortium
www.tamupress.com

First Edition

CONTENTS

It's my bird, I will let it go
yes I know
and then I won't sing no more
      -KRISTIAN MATSSON

We could see the sadness as a gift and still
feel too heavy to hold
      -ADRIANNE LENKER

ONE

Controlled Burn

To the north
they have set fire
to a thousand acres
of a very real forest
to prevent future fires.

Walking through the ash
it makes sense to him
the many ways
we handle a decadence
not our own.

The trees survive
their bark seared
but intact
the ground charred and gray
with the exhalation of hope.

It makes sense to him
burning down this fear
before the greater pain sets in
singing praise in a cloud of smoke
watching the animals flee.

Foreign

This day.
Looking for the goat lost
over that hill. And finding
the gun.
Learning the music
of a spent cartridge.
And perfecting it.

There is no burial
for the body
without looking at the body.
We have abandoned the field
anyway, unwilling to dig.

There is only this brief pause of noon.
Shadowless. The smell of rust lifting
off the orchard floor.

Wind-knocked peaches feeding
the ancient grass bordering
every entryway, hungry.

A static hand upon your neck.
The miraculous erasure of home.
Catching your breath. Good
child. Good.
                    Again.

Because They Hunger, They Take

Starlings overtake
the bird feeder
pass through this way
stay a few days then carry on.

Their metallic coats shimmer.
The heads of grass along the forest fringe
about to drop into womb
go unnoticed.

Mourning doves linger
beneath the basket of seeds
waiting, discussing applications of empathy
or economics, what poverty means

if it means anything to them
in their colony on the coast.
Waiting. And the starlings eat.
They eat it all.

Birth

Trying to explain away the existence
of existence and becoming
lost in the etymology of *bird*.

There is a way to walk
through ripened hay fields
without noticing the hay—

this is called today & now.
The day marching through us
as we hurry to find its end.

The gift of *temporary*. The act
of making toast one thousand mornings
without contentment. Because of the idea

of hunger. Because time moves smoothly
through the infinite delight
of perfecting the unnecessary

he is painting a new barn
for his father. Working hard enough
to buy a truck for next fall.

Thinking, *This is important.*
This is what it takes. The luminosity
of sunlight within the walls

becoming less real than its heat.
The honesty of a hummingbird
exhausting itself in these rafters.

Believing in the always goodness of upwards.
That heaven is only over our heads.
Unaware of the gaping door below.

Perhaps unwilling.
Somewhere there is death. And somewhere else
there is birth. But mostly

a broad postponement. A simple denial
that we circle the sun. Instead believing
it comes to us. Again & again.

Because of worth. And value.
And life. The unbearable affirmation of *life*.

Border Guard

Because the deer were too plentiful
we chained up an old hound dog

> at the back of the field
> to protect asparagus throughout summer.

In the day you could see him chasing shade.
At night a whimper, a bark

> a small thing dying inside of teeth.
> After school I'd carry each day

buckets of food and water
across the acres

> my small frame straining
> under the unbalanced weight.

Water is a heavy thing
to deliver. I'd give what I'd brought

> speak some kindness
> and cross the land again

dinner waiting on a worn table.
And the dog would watch until I vanished

beyond the curve of field
and the deer would wait

and the harvest was never enough anyways.
Because the deer had such great need

and the line was only imaginary
in fall our guns came out.

We Are Still Building Beach Houses

Surely God is sitting
on the ocean floor
waiting

for our small act
of consenting
to time

knowing the sudden loss
of any object resonates
for years not knowing

what a day holds
beyond postponement
beyond asking for more

of what never quite was
imagining ourselves robbed
we invent hope even at sunset

which is why water
lives inside water
and we call it a body.

Retirement Plan

I walk the path up
to the house I do not own
each day in time

for what my body
can yet receive. The gourds outside
the door already unraveling

into mush because of routine.
I worry about the mind.
What I'm trying to work out

is whether my silence
is the newest absence
I haven't waded through yet.

So I hum in rhythm
with the knife and bread
and the hour goes

and another day unravels.
Down the path
away

from what I don't want
to matter. Time and how
we believe it moves.

Phenomenological Summertime Cocktail

I have yet learned to be
though I look for you who has.

Listening to the sound of cattle
and the song of their shit in the pasture.

They won't be here in Spring
like so many things.

I am breathing in the air of old roof shingles
tar and decades of their attempt at definition

now being removed from a shape
that was once our home.

We think of what we want.
This the flower, that the weed.

In the dirt.
Everything in the dirt.

The dirt which we know
by pressing our fluids into.

Hoping for sense, searching
for the border of a field

that by explaining its shape
we've said something about ourselves.

Walk through the pasture
and become pasture.

Wade into the lake
and become the idea of a line.

Singing, Even Now

We become accustomed
to this slow fading out
inevitably.

Our hinges dry
the foliage of the mind
drowning as the waters gently rise.

But we can yet walk
along the streets and see
a face we love.

It's more than a joy
that quick flashing
and gone.

It's not postponing
the assault
of the body.

It's not leaving the hospital
after the cure
the bright day waiting.

It could be
noticing that cigarette butt
white against the gray of the parking lot

ground down to its idea.
Knowing someone smoked it
with their wonderful lungs

that they arrived
at the end of a thing
successfully.

That they left it here.
That they were here
where you stand.

That they exist despite
their familiarity
with living

as you do
alone
in none of it.

Natural Occurrence

It just so happens
the vine is faster
than the tree.

The day's end and I
have yet to speak
a word out loud.

But inward
my spirit is climbing
the body.

I know in time this scaffolding
will wither, that a forest falls
into itself eventually.

Even love crawls upward
from the desolation
of the individual

the vine and its hope
strangling the hope
of another.

Cost of Living

Am here with the day
and its gentle dying.

The dog cleaning herself
on the couch loudly. Am thinking
of this maintenance
we've perfected.

Autumn, inevitably.
What apples remain
rotting towards something
misunderstood as waste.

There has always been enough.
Tomorrow rolls along
because of this excess.
In spite of it.

Our time split by memory
split by the desire
to simply forget
knowledge and its birdsong.

Of course we exist.
We make this so
by giving ourselves
over to it.

Storm Newly Common

The sound as branches
because the pressure is constant
leave behind the one thing
they've always known.

Tonight ten thousand houses
will lose power. Standing outside
shouting you will forget
the purpose of voice.

Some of the birds weather it
by existing tomorrow
the rest remain a song.
And tomorrow another storm.

Branches like likely children
deposited in a field.
Like a sentence unfinished
if you want it.
        Paint on a wall.
        A much too well known.

The Sky is a Frame as We Need It

In late morning
they unearth bulbs
before the frost
while this earth slants finally
enough for the work.

Gathered in bushels
and placed in the basement to dry.
One reheats the coffee
while the other makes a list
of each event.

A thousand years from now
it's hopefully raining
is a prayer they hum
to avoid what they think
they know of tomorrow.

Bulbs asleep beneath their home
coffee drifting from hot
to warm and reheated into bitterness.
The earth slanted like an idea
like how they wish they could dance

in a darkness
outside the body
outside the reluctant memory
that darkness is defined
as little more than absence.

I Hope This Finds Me Well

Last night a deer
his antlers bare
approached the concrete slab
where I sat and finished
a drink in the dark.

I was pretending to care
about starlight
when he broke through
the fallen branches. The echo
of his hooves, even now.

We were both lost
in giving up slowly.
Acknowledging each other
by looking away.
Perfectly kind.

Rain When You Want It

He no longer sets
the coffee pot before bed
as the imminence of pleasure
keeps him from sleep.

By this time of year
the green tomatoes
will never make it to red
and still the vine says *wait*.

He nearly can walk on water
if it's cold enough
which is a gift
he eats with fear.

Wait. It's a fine sadness holding
these smaller movements of joy
as consolation. The coffee, for a moment
too wonderfully hot to drink.

The vine and its fruit
cascading into failure.

Marriage II

It was a too hard touching
of the thing unseen.

We'd travel to the coast
and stop short

because we had forgotten
how to walk

on water
when it's calm.

All those storms
and tossing waves sure

simple but that calmness
came and drowned us.

Good Poverty

Near the corner of property
now overgrown with black locusts
that writhe in the lack of wind

these ruins
of a barn once housed
too few cattle and heavy lanterns in morning
the waning mystery of darkness chasing
after purpose amid the broken laughter
of children learning about the movement of hay
through time

the great effort of it all
I come here often
as we all do
searching among these old stones
for that loud bucket of fresh milk.

Side Work

Grandfather witching for water.
Divining dad called it
because God and fear inherited.

The effort of wood and its silence.
The rod's graceful dip
dependent upon what we choose to believe.

He'd pass the land slow, eyes nearly closed.
The drill team waiting with their monstrous rig.
A different silence.

What amazed me most
was not how he always struck water
but how he found the perfectly forked branch

a slender tool allowing
men to forget
the heaviness of our terror.

Religion

He walks her direction
surrounded by sunlight.

The family watches. Cold beer
and condensation along their hands.

Hot dogs. Vague talk of football
or the divine strength of a dollar bill

anything so long as it distracts
into the freedom of night.

Tomorrow the lawn will be mowed.
An overstuffed box of recycling

pressed near the curb where streetlights sing
muted fellowship with bats in flight.

Field Work

He wakes back bent into a kind of platform
for what is meant to be goodness.

Heat of the sun in the soil near his face.

Imagine wind noticing itself.
That kind of silence

each morning. Across the field a body
of another, watching.

What Hegel said about two souls.
Each holding a seed

in their loose fists. Terrified
to let go, knowing the need

to sow. To join that patch-work quilt
landscape to something.

Receiving the fly-over-fuck-you
gift of nothing, despite the effort.

Back to bed, the soil cooling.
Again, again.

Terrified of claiming
of being claimed.

Overture

Preparing green beans
beneath the absurd pulse
of migrating gulls

pressing through the tail skirts
of an already receding moment.
The breath of their wings

off the brim of the lake.
Tossing aside the snips.
Intentionally aiming for ground.

Taking the time. Fabricating
within the body
these quiet instruments.

Tuning the self for the performance
of living. Terribly.
Convincing this body to leave

the person it loves.
Charming the heart to drown itself
for the sake of an absence

in the morning. These birds
lost in their performance
of certainty. Finally

revealing the evening stars
as the affirmation of what was.
There is only ebb.

You find yourself
jettisoned outward
hands full of the neighbor's harvest.

Behind you
in a warm house,
that familiar flesh is boiling water.

But first the snapping of these things.
First the emptying of these hands.
And then the orchestra of the body.

Owned

Cliff swallows and the certainty
of their absence at dusk

something known, amen.

The field and its abundance of taking.
A broke-down tractor

finally gathering

that space before starlight
and its hunger.

Sparseness as promise

of more to come.
He is standing in a barn

a dead man built slowly.

Grappling in the darkness
for a tattered manual.

This day, that month

and the years, dear Lord
we lack the time

for disappointment.

Cliff swallows preparing the day
for the nest to come. Each day

        piling upon another until *nest*.

The pages in his hands
shaking only slightly

        because enough.

Leaning on air he reads
illuminated by the light

        of his own body.

The roundness of night.
Even now the dew unhindered.

What About Ambition, Its Hunger?

Bread not because of butter
but wheat planted beneath sparrows
and my grandfather in a grave

the wind no longer
at his hand in the wheat
this summer or the next

nor the promise that bed gives
that turning over and awake
there is somehow more

instead at night, exhausted
we taste honesty
and spend the day forgetting it.

What we do instead.
Postponing a thing like love
until worn out with age

fortress of the mind finally broken
we allow ourselves to witness
when the heart says yes.

The luxury, the artifice gone.
The apple not sliced and sugared
into pie, but frozen in winter

on the branch and pressed into wine.
The promise of more
finally terrifying. Finally too much.

Birthday

The next village over
and another man
who is also afraid to sleep.

His gray dog near the bed.
With each pause in its breathing he hears
the promise of chaos, all the stars of heaven
careening towards the house
so he walks through the doors, instead.

Outside he measures the honesty of hay
with bared feet. Through the window
a radio delivering some local midnight violin.

It reminds him of sixty years
and then the suddenness.
It reminds him of this moment
the moon-soaked resistance
of alfalfa underfoot

the nearness of death each night
the hostility of living in spite of love
the acres of darkness ready for harvest.

Returning From Sunday Service Sometime, Sometime Ago

I have the boots.
The broken fence. The timed charge of a cicada, a tilting
hawk, some peripheral beast. Cow
in the backyard. An occasional car

pausing, a golden caprice classic.
My dad's hands within the cow. Somehow.
Tying a slender rope to something within,
somehow. Each time she would seize up and grunt

he would lean back and pull. And for a moment
the arch of his back was empyrean.
Eventually the rope. Slick with mystery.
Then hooves. A kind of body. The frothy mess.

And the whole time, in each pull
his heavy boots cut away the earth
beneath him. That grip upon the rope.
Those hands. Ruined.

Those hands
should be my hands.
I have the boots. Yes.
But I've lost the pull.

Call Me Out of the Woods

The long faded grass
of what was once a moving field.
Oak. A break in the wind.
This knife moving

opening the deer.
Holding the liver, the heart
each cooling, each silent
when I ask about love.

Now, its eyes closed
even the steam of the body
drifting away.
How else will we know?

TWO

An Origin Story

Rain last night.
Today sun.
And always the clock.

I have become terribly aware of my skin
the newly overabundant spread
of chairs in my living room

        these too many wine glasses
        used only to trap mice
        and set them free.

One must learn the use of low lighting.
Of many tiny lamps.

        It is a heaviness
        that forces down the specter.

Trust the familiar thunder of music
and wait for it to become a new silence.

        What is hard to explain
        is how good it is.
        Like vegetables.
        The fiber of a muffin.

You must invest in a glance beyond
the pall of the glass and zinc coat,

the copper wire. Through the wall, the walk-in closet
next door. A pressed suit. The neighbor's water
running in the shower. The screech of a closing valve.

Tomorrow
let it be unpredictable.

> Water or light.
> Wind against skin.
> Birds perhaps learning
> a new dance against the pane
> of your painted-shut window.
> A hand at the door
> the click of a key
> a knob turning into voice.

Sermon at a Wedding on a Michigan Farm

If all the bailing twine
in this barn
is not enough

to hold a neck
if you can grip
the tail of a rooster

before it lifts its wings
and beats itself
over the roof

into a nonsense
of declarations
if your grandmother told jokes

between each of her stillbirths
and your father grew up
believing death

was an exhalation of joy
then perhaps together
we hold the shovel

the excavation of memory
forgotten in the work
in the bowels of a field

the warmth of breakfast
worn out too many rows back
the softness of a bed

and what happens in a bed
and how the cattle bed down
in mud and dew

how the kids fork cow shit
through a too small window
how the shit is necessary

for the crops
for the new used-shoes
the wire that holds up

the car's back bumper
on its way to church
and the weekly tithe

love maybe even
or the forces of biology
a reason to leave the twine

on the barn floor
next to the shovel
next to the frightened hen

huddled over her clutch hoping
that God will blow the roof off
and tell her she's done alright.

Marriage

They arrive each summer
at Lake Ontario

    leap out of hot vehicles
    their dog chasing behind

as they race to the shore
where fifteen-year-old lifeguards

    forbid them from swimming
    beyond the buoyed rope

a few yards out.
So they wade

    the water lapping
    against their thighs.

And all that lake.
Geese overhead

    pushing their wings
    against a substance

we confuse with something
known. Like religion

    or love.
    Perhaps what it should be

were the world flat enough
were we able to move these bodies

    without obstacle
    without the need to look back

and correct our course.
We are not permitted to see

    what pries waves up from the deep
    shoves them across the canvas

what pushes their thought
against the shore.

    Only in their collapse
    we begin to understand

absence as illusion.
They will return home

    to the house, the adequate mailbox
    the neglected backyard chickens.

But for now their dog runs along the shore
barking at the waves

    not because they approach
    but because they approach again.

Before Divorce

The road continues up the hill
paved, winding through hot trees
and ditches.

Most days I walk
to the bare top.
There is a horse ranch

and too many acres
to look upon.
Also, the sun often unobscured.

Horses standing about grazing
kicking godly into a movement
that feels like promise

an agreement between beast and earth
that by pressing against each other
they arrive at existence.

In the dust, beetles leaping
from blades of grass, through the silence
after each hoof.

The horses, lost in what we want to be joy
halt before reaching the fence
where a current of knowledge waits.

Not the knowledge of gain or loss.
The knowledge of this is enough.
Not what we want acceptance to be

but what it often is.
You and I holding up a god, an idea
merely by our shared presence
merely by acknowledging the space
where a god is not.
Too many acres to look upon

and suddenly too alone.
Back down the hill, back to the home.
Back, back.

After

Stumbling in every moment
of silence erasing

what your breath felt like
from across the orchard

I push this furniture
around the room

the borrowed couch against window glass
the table where the bed once was

and the bed outside
push till it all feels right

the carpet torn
the coffee pot shattered

leaves and slugs
and other strangers

in the blankets with me
beneath these trees.

Grief

Up here in April
winter remains
in the shade of the woods
waiting for a larger portion
of what everyone else
has already accepted.

Winter

breaking on occasion into the rare
smile of a friend or stranger or bird

stumbling through the snow I refuse
to shovel I have been alone an entire year

and I want to see the drifts build
I want to understand accumulation

even if it must exist outside this body
often it's only a river

that separates one language from another
the surface of the water broken

the mirror broken, the broken promise
that a river separates when it sutures

a common greeting lost in the span
of so many watery yards

how we take for granted the daily
nod of a stranger

the gentle downward bob of the chin
the grace of awkward eye contact

because proximity
forgetting currents push all things down river

forgetting that reaching for shore
it is dry and claimed

traveling further north
to witness of all things the effort

of time in certain leaves
in a certain season

this year
and the next

it is not time
not the boredom of the clock

not the failure to complete the dishes
the body the stretch of rocks that were a home

not the leaf unfurling in sunlight
but the bird on the branch

at the end of every story
a bird in the brief silence

before a bullet a loaf of bread
slowly pulled from the oven next door

winter arrives on time
these days after a long walk

the dog lies down
her hind legs bind up

keep her from standing
so she drags her body

across the rough floor
each time I look at her

it all arrives in time
the aging of whisky

for another generation
the gathering dust of pig skin

for the use of jello
but first the pig

first its too quick walk from womb
to our invention of womb

this snow dusting the earth
piling up

sometimes for weeks
sometimes meeting the ground

and melting at once
honest in what it wants

i am learning about prayer again
how it operates within the roots

of its own silence
how the rind of any gourd

grows round a thing soft
takes the sun's beating

how the fruit rots
from within that thick shell

deceiving even itself
slowly softening too late

around what now is emptiness
we are accidentally alive

accidentally stumbling through it
each of has at one point caught our toe

against some uneven rise in the sidewalk
where were we going

in that moment of fall and catching
we laugh or curse out loud

grow red-faced looking about hoping
that no one saw & somehow disappointed

that indeed we moved without witness
that moment that crack in space

laugh or curse
i awake each day

to the too much goodness of eggs coffee
the lack of being seen

and what makes air
define our boundaries of kindness

the many winds turning
dried leaves against the window

the window and the leaves
the cracked shells and coffee grounds

each day turned into heap
steadily harvesting entropy

dear glory and decay
we were too young

and death too far away
to remind us of anything

beyond arm's reach
even tomorrow

forgotten
so we let the garden crawl

over the wall at night
left the windows cracked open

breathed well we could
breath of hand looking for summer

this soil turned enough
to earn what we choose to forfeit

this is dinner
this is tooth

on tooth emptiness
the rooster unable to interpret

god's hands into a breath
a call to forget

our need for movement
distance love and all its great failures

the pitch of the roof of the barn
imperfect but steady in this wind

because the steel wheelbarrow
carries only a sheen of rain

the promise of rust
and what more

no one needs
is the lie we bed into

inventing the dream
that woke us now standing

at my front door lost
in the thought of keys

i am no longer able to love you
birds at the empty feeder waiting

the empty sack of seeds
in the recycling the bin at the curb

knocked over for weeks
and this locked door

this intensity of keys
how we hope to live long enough

to begin to hope for death
how these birds know loss

is not the broken wing
but the absence of sky

the earth tilts for this
the metamorphose of precipitation

how a thing changes
as it falls

great boughs of white pine in michigan
torn from the trunk under the weight

of snow the collection of a million
singular actions what the wheat farmer

will pray for in a month's time
it is good this sadness

is my own invention
i want most to become

your stranger
to find the great oceanic noise

of where a heart once was
barely drowned out

by the sound of snow falling
trying to fall

the wind pushing then lifting
flirting with gravity

then a crash a departure
in the thickness of july

you can find honeybees
resting along the doorsteps

of their cabins in the orchard
you will see the quick rise

and fall of their bodies exhausted
meanwhile highways of pilots

loaded with pollen
stream in and out of the hive

you can stand amidst that current
unharmed unnoticed they sting

out of fear and they do not fear you
but the summer and its ending

alone listen for it
the approaching loss of purpose

what the sun does to trees
eventually

the hope of a stone
how terrible it is to know anything

Body as a Home Unknown

Down this street
or the event otherwise;
culmination. Of course.
Beyond intention.

Fruit
of the word
of who we aim to be

too often succeeding.

Bird in flight.
and the other non-bird.

THREE

It is Easier to Talk About What the Body Remembers

Despite its fragile skin
a frog survives underground for entire winters.

We once wondered what their dreams looked like.
If they were actually alive or just resurrected.

How they know when and how to travel upwards
the way trees seem so certain

about at least one thing. And we invent envy instead.
I am thinking of village elders wrapping religion

around their bodies like ancient gowns of taffeta.
The frog hides its soul all winter long and is blessed

with thaw and sex. I want you to notice
these cotton woods, how they toss out their hope

in waves of leaving. Stagnancy is death to the tree.
Distance always the goal. In the cool morning

of Venice. Empty streets. Birds unfurling their praise.
Marco Polo's father asking how far will you go

& how far are you willing to go? And opens his book
as the first customer of the day

comes to him.
I am thinking of honesty and trying to conjure rain

only mustering wine. Is this what Christ meant for?
Not the wedding nor the spectators

but the need of an excuse for tomorrow?
The crowd shouting out

> *there must be something in the dirt*
> *there must be enough heat underneath*
> *to keep dead things alive*

Forgetting the wind running through their hair
brushing against the subtle brokenness of their skin.

Not Decadent But Simple

Outside this morning routine
I forget birds exist.
Apple blossoms wet without noticing.
Their lives not bound
by any pleasure.

Tearing apart yesterday's bread
with sudden hands. Running
each piece through left over
bacon grease. Still hot.
The body cannot recall

the present. There is something
kind about hunger. How it feeds us.
Or doesn't. Allowing us
to forget the source. Wanting
to say I love you

audible enough for only the intended
to hear. She thinks him embarrassed.
He clumsily aims at intimacy.
This confusion makes holy
what we choose not to describe—

Midwestern. Searching for the job
for the family for the job.
Beginning to understand the need
to understand something. Feigning
the knowledge of crows

on a man-made wire.
Working through the engine of existence.
Earning a thing like cancer
or bubble gum. Despite everything
waking is still mandatory. Glorious

and brief. The suffering here
seeming more distant than the suffering
over there. A canary in the shaft
freed of its cage. Flying deeper.
Confused by the paternal warmth

and widening darkness.
Assured, till the end, of deliverance.
Faithfully traveling through life
toward the beginning of something
unnecessary though wanted simply.

Second-Hand Knowledge

Breaking apart limbs
for the wrong kind of sap

drinking it up learning
of lack before the final good.

Our eagerness for tomorrow
as taproot of failure anticipated.

Rows in the field made straight
so we can identify the effort

and hold it close at night.
A morning collection of eggs.

Washing from each slowly
its imperfection of roundness.

The subtle violence sheer
through a curtain soft window light.

Thoughts of nothing
as medicine for everything.

Replacing our loss
with a broken kindness

each day promises a sapling
the shade of its origin.

Dipping For Osmeridae, Upper Peninsula Michigan 1988

They make a fire
along the riverbank
to keep their hands warm
and for something to do.

Wading out to their knees
they dip for smelt.
Their long nets straining
with moving gems.
Enough to fill a bucket each.

The smoke from the fire
rolls beneath their bodies
and will live within those heavy coats
for months.

Later they'll dump the buckets into a truck
and go back for another wading out deeper
dipping the net again and again
until it becomes fruitless

and the trucks depart
and the embers cool
until some wind
makes a god of them.

The End of Self-Help

I am building a garden wall
to fill up that emptiness
within me that was mentioned.

Carefully caught my fingers
between the slamming
of a few stones, as suggested.

The birds watch. And the dog
moves from the sun to the shade
and back again. The day goes.

I may fade before it's all finished—
birds free to examine where I've moved
the earth, the possibility of a worm

which will be good enough.
Check on the dog. Plant those tomatoes.
Talk with someone of their taste.

Cheap Beer

If there is less rain this year
or if the grain prices get goofy
because a couple dudes

want a bit more
more farmers will kill
themselves easily enough.

We are rarely taught
to speak of it
if it hurts.

To listen for the wind
to die down so we can
spray the fields free

of life unwanted, yes,
but to hear a voice lost
and looking is the static

of a universe that slams
our prayers against each other
without a sound.

Taught, each one of us, to use
the many guns we grew up with
like shovels or pitch forks.

Taught how to be safe.
Not to point them
at each other

or ourselves.
The danger understood, respected even
learned and tucked away for another day

when we're older and caught
in that self-built trap of love
when the rain is slow

and billionaires drink
that good shit on the moon.

Belladonna on the Farm

At dawn the great grandfather left
to deal with crows in the field.
He had prepared a wash tin of chucked corn
soaking overnight in arsenic.
This morning he consecrated the ground
with hallowed kernels, with bare hands. And then
watched the feast from beneath an alder tree.
Watched realization ignite in clumsy wings
and the leaping tremble of death
stretch out across the purple screen.
Watched the crashing of feathers,
from within the shadows of stalks,
from within the shade of fence posts his father built
a thousand years ago.
Watched the fox and wolf gather.
And clapping his hands, walking home.

Pastor

He is in the church moving
among the pews slow
with his abundance of time.
It is early. Before the dew
is burnt off and the day presses
into its subtle chaos
of children and untimed clapping.

He checks to make sure
the doors are unlocked.
Turns their knobs many times
as though he were figuring them out.
The mechanics. A small thing
moving the larger, a wall
diminishing into a thought.

His shoes are tied, his hair
nearly dry. Today the belt
with the buckle he likes.
Eventually people will arrive
and he is waiting
but not for them.

How to Believe

I've spent the day struggling
to split wood
for a fire I do not need
though I want to need it.

It's a lucky moment.
To sweat with the sun
and cold clear air.
This is how I forget

what I choose
to look away from.
With the effort of rhythm
the blade sometimes glancing

into the dirt. Which is good, too.
What I would say
were there a crowd
between each swing I won't

say now. I will earn the sweat
but not the fire.
The wood is passive in the act.
I tell myself this.

Before Death

A bird in the kitchen
this morning.
It was enough.
A song among tangerine bowls.
Near the open window
atop the butcher-block table—
grapefruit
       a spoon.
            Unequivocal.
Peering out into darkness
for sunrise.
Knowing
it will blind.

Too much.
       Hallelujah.
       Even the seeds.

NOTES AND ACKNOWLEDGMENTS

I am indebted to the many teachers, in school & out, who taught me the value of language, writing, & art. Special thanks to Jim Stuart, John Wolff, Maria Mazziotti Gillan, Joe Weil, & Leslie Heywood for their encouragement & guidance, & for their friendship.

Over the years, I have been fortunate to befriend or become acquainted with some of the greatest humans & writers. Much thanks to those who have helped me, or inspired me, or challenged me, or all of it: Adam J. Gellings, Elizabeth Dark, Adam Clay, Dante Di Stefano, Nate Arida, Brian Kamsoke, Eniko Vaghy, Jay McMahan, Shelley Wong, Solmaz Sharif, Claire Olsen, Leah Umansky & so many.

The beautiful cover image is a painting originally done in black-China ink by Twotma (Aimée Pedezert). Thank you!

I spent some years working as an adjunct instructor and bartender (as so many have). Thanks to my past co-workers for your friendship & conversation. A number of these poems began behind the bar on those rare slow days.

Those summers in Michigan. Work on the farm. Sweat & play. My dad wanting his kids to be better readers than he was. My mom taking my brother & me to the local libraries. How we labored through *Hooked on Phonics*. But intention. Those winters, too. I need to give thanks to the place: Lake Michigan & the many rivers. The fields & forests. The secret vernal ponds & their bacchanalian frogs. How place insists that you look, slowly. Or deeply. Mason County. A barn is a universe. A bale of hay slowly rotting in the mow, even now.

Thanks to Sarah for your love & honest support & for encouraging me to be me. Michael & Alexis: the siblings I was born with & the siblings I would have chosen. Again & again. My colleagues at Central State University who have given me a new home & warm encouragement. Brendan Shaw for your kindness & guidance.

Thank you to the schools & institutions that have helped me along the way: Mason County Central Schools, West Shore Community College, Western Michigan University, Wichita State University, & Binghamton University. Thanks to the Keynon Review for providing me with the Peter Taylor Fellowship. Thanks to the Glen Arbor Arts Center (& the wonderful people who work there) for giving me a space amongst their artist-in-residences.

Some of these poems first appeared in my chapbook *the body as passage*. Thank you, Elise Jajuga & Open Palm Print, for making that a possibility.

Thanks to Kim Verhines & Mallory LeCroy & Stephen F. Austin State University Press for giving this collection a home.

To Dill Eleanor. The best. Who knows where I'd be without you.

Much thanks to the following journals, magazines, & presses, & the hardworking editors, readers, & staff, that published the following work, sometimes in earlier versions:

Aperçus: "Because They Hunger, They Take"
Banango Street: "Foreign"
Best New Poets: "Foreign"
Cleaver: "Field Work"
The Colorado Review: "Not Decadent But Simple"
The Dialogist: "Birthday"
EcoThe Review: "Owned"
Friends: "Most Evenings"
Funny Looking Dog Quarterly: "Sermon at a Wedding on a Michigan Farm"
Foothill: "Belladonna on the Farm"
Mikrokosmos: "Border Guard" *&* "Picnic Arrival"
Nixes Mate Review: "Grief"
North American Review: "Side Work"
Ovenbird Poetry: "Rehabilitation of the Self, A Process"
Open Palm Print: "Overture" *&* "Returning from Sunday Service Sometime, Sometime Ago"
Prometheus Dreaming: "Marriage"
Qua Magazine: "It is Easier to Talk About What the Body Remembers*"
Rabbit Catastrophe Review: "Body as a Home Unknown"
Tammy: "Origin Story"
Third Coast: "Birth"
TYPO: "Good Poverty" *&* "Winter"

* "It is Easier to Talk About What the Body Remembers" was originally co-written with Haley Nieboer.

NATHAN LIPPS is the author of the chapbook *the body as passage* (Open Palm Print, 2019). A recipient of a Peter Taylor Fellowship, an Excellence award in Research (SUNY Binghamton), and a Poetry Fellowship (Wichita State University), Nathan's work has appeared in *Best New Poets, Bombay Literary Magazine, Cleaver, EcoTheo Review, Colorado Review, North American Review, Third Coast, TYPO,* and *Verse Daily.* Born and raised along the rural coast of western Michigan, he currently lives in Ohio and teaches at Central State University.

Printed in the USA
CPSIA information can be obtained
at www.ICGtesting.com
LVHW051140030424
776227LV00004B/15